Date Due

Hensall			
JUL 3			
AUG 7			
JUL 2			
AUG 2 0 1985			
MAR 1 4 1987			
JUN 0 2 1990			
AUG 2 2 1995			
AUG 1 3			
SEP 1 5 2000			

The
Cabot
Trail

The Cabot Trail

David Street

gage PUBLISHING LIMITED
Toronto · Vancouver · Calgary · Montreal

Design by Richard Whyte

Canadian Cataloguing in Publication Data

Street, David, 1947-
The Cabot Trail

ISBN O-7715-9450-X bd. ISBN O-7715-9451-8 pa.

1. Cabot Trail – Description and travel – Views.
2. Cape Breton Island, N.S. – Description and travel – Views.
I. Title.

FC2343.4.S77   917.16′9′00222   C79-094283-6
F1039.C2S77

Printed in Canada
1 2 3 4 BP 82 81 80 79

To my wife Maggie.
Together we shared the friendliness of Cape Breton.

Fisherman's Prayer

God give me the grace to catch a fish
So big that even I,
When speaking of it afterwords
May never need to lie.

Preface

This is not a tourist guidebook. Rather it is a portrait, an introduction, an invitation, if you like, to one of the most beautiful natural journeys in North America—the Cabot Trail. One hundred and eighty-four miles long, the Cabot Trail is a tar and stone-covered roadway looping around the northern finger of Cape Breton Island in the maritime province of Nova Scotia. My intention while photographing this book was to capture the views of the land as seen from the Trail and with very few exceptions all the photographs were taken from the road's edge. I also wanted to show the character of the people who live along the Trail, for although a spectacular tourist route, the Trail also serves as a lifeline for the area's residents.

They are a true island people, introspective and reserved, yet they are generous and will offer the stranger warm hospitality just as long as he refrains from asking questions that invade their personal privacy. It would take a generation to be considered an "insider" on Cape Breton. Even so, a visitor who is interested in avoiding the usual tourist traps will find that if he takes the time to stop and chat with the local people, the old men with rugged faces will share the lore of the land with him, the boys fishing from a dock will readily discuss the day's luck. From these conversations the visitor will begin to understand the style of life so energetically and proudly preserved, and begin to get the true feeling of the land. The forests, the space of open fields, the shadows of the mountains, the clean scent of running water will begin to work its magic in a world where the joy of small pleasures is so often lost.

One of the special appeals for travellers like myself, is that the Cabot Trail, unlike so many scenic routes with vistas and roads laid out by engineers and appraisers, passes through working communities where day-to-day life exists. As it winds its way around the bays, over mountains, through the forests and ambling valley fields, the Cabot Trail is a magical mystery tour. Like Alice in Wonderland, the traveller will experience fantasies and thrills, knowing all the while that he will in the end, return to the beginning. It is a journey that affects all who take it—an adventure that leaves you able to "see" the wind and "hear" the sun rise.

Introduction

To understand Cape Breton, the land, the heritage and traditions embodied in a journey around the Cabot Trail, one must go back to the very beginning—to the pre-Cambrian era when the undulating land mass of the Island of Cape Breton was formed. As one travels along the coastal section of the Trail near Cap Rouge on the shores of the Gulf, the eye is entranced by the varying red, black, green and silver of the base rocks. There are granites, quartzes, schists and crystalline limestone and seldom are they available in such visible forms and combinations.

Some four hundred million years ago, other rock formations were created by the cooling off of the masses of igneous rock. A constant folding and breaking or fracturing of the land continued on, together with the ever-present effects of the climatic conditions. During the carboniferous age three hundred million years ago, coal in its early form of gypsum was deposited, later to be first mined by the French in 1720.

Looked at from a statistical point of view, the Cabot Trail is a two-lane, tar-topped highway in excellent condition, which stretches for a hundred and eighty-four miles around the northern tip or "finger" of Cape Breton Island. The main urban centre, Baddeck, is a little more than eleven hundred miles from Toronto and nine hundred and eighty miles from New York City.

On the western side of the Island, the Trail runs alongside the waters of the Gulf of St. Lawrence and on the eastern side it edges up against the Atlantic Ocean. The forested and mountainous landscape of the area is sparsely populated. In fact, there are fewer than forty villages and communities located along the Trail's route, some of them holding no more than a dozen people. In many of these villages, the Trail forms the main street and is very much a lifeline for supply and communication.

There are four major mountains to cross on the Trail: Cape Smokey is the steepest climbing 1,200 feet in one and a third miles, then North Mountain, 1,460 feet, MacKenzie, 1,222 feet, and French Mountain the highest at 1,492 feet, overlooking the Gulf of St. Lawrence.

With the exception of the modern-day tourist trade, the main industries and employment of the area are fishing, lumbering and farming. There is also a growing handicrafts industry and a number of attempts have been made recently to expand small industries. In Cheticamp a small metalwork manufacturing industry has been started and a shipyard that once built fishing boats now supplies materials for a growing house-building trade. Although most of the heavy traffic on the Trail is during the tourist seasons in the summer and fall, the road is kept cleared during the heavy winter snows when it truly becomes a lifeline, protecting the communities along its route from isolation. Indeed, with the exception of some of the mountain sections, the direction the Cabot Trail took, when it was completed in 1932, closely followed the old paths and wagon tracks trodden down by generations of inhabitants visiting from one village to another.

The town of Baddeck, the biggest and most prosperous community, is generally accepted as the start and finish of the Cabot Trail, even though the Trail actually by-passes Baddeck by a few miles. The Trail on the eastern route along St. Anns Bay, weaves in and out of woodland, alongside fields and around the bays of the Atlantic. The main community on the eastern side is congregated around Ingonish, a group of small villages sharing the cove and overshadowed by Cape Smokey. This mountain, the first on the route of the Trail, gets its name from the wisps of cloud that cling to its twelve-hundred foot summit in the mists of the early morning.

In the north section the Trail borders the Cape Breton Highlands National Park whose perimeter it becomes. This national park was opened in 1936 and although there have been a number of new roadways and walking trails cut into the woodland, great care is taken to maintain its natural wild state.

Heading west along the top of the Island the Trail heads toward the village of Cape North in the shadow of the Aspy mountain chain. After leaving the park region at Petit Etang, the route takes one through the picturesque village of Cheticamp, the centre of the Acadian culture and certainly one of the more prosperous communities on the Trail. If you follow the Margaree Valley inland past the Village of Margaree Forks, supposedly named after the Marguerite, a local wildflower, the Trail then winds back through farm and forest land to Baddeck.

The earliest known inhabitants of Cape Breton were the Micmac Indians and we have little knowledge of their history although an excavated site at Little Narrows is yielding artifacts covering a span of approximately three thousand years. We do know that they were a nomadic people who hunted the plentiful game of the forests in the winter months. In the spring and summer they moved to the shores where they fished in the coastal waters. From all accounts it appears that they were not an aggressive people and lived simple and peaceful lives which were to change dramatically after the European immigrants arrived.

Later, during the seemingly constant struggle between the French and British for sovereignty of the island, the Micmacs were generally regarded as allies of the French. They were recruited as guides, traded furs and sometimes helped raid New England settlements. Regarded as ferocious warriors in battle, it was hoped that fear of their raids would ensure the loyalty of the Acadian people to the French flag.

When the British won control of Cape Breton, the status of the Micmacs declined drastically. After the cession of Acadia to Britain the hostilities of the Micmac continued and it was not until 1779 that the last warfare between them and the British ceased. The British considered them a hindrance to settlement and cleared them off their land. Although in 1852 the British Commissioner for Crown Lands granted titles to Indians for land held by them at the time, most of their good land had already been taken from them. Today the modern Micmacs are about 2,500 in number, living in five reserves on Cape Breton.

Whether in fact, John Cabot was the first European to walk the shores of Cape Breton is highly debatable. It is possible that Cabot didn't sight Cape Breton at all but a promontory off the Maine or Newfoundland shores instead. But historians agree that it could have been Cape Breton and the island has claimed him for their own. A plaque erected in the north of Victoria County bears this inscription:

On 24th June 1497 in the "Matthew" out of Bristol England, with a crew of eighteen men, John Cabot discovered the continent of North America. His landfall 'first land seen' was in this vicinity and is believed to have been the lofty headlands of north Cape Breton.

The discovery of the continent had not been Cabot's main ambition. After persuading England's King Henry VII to allow him "full and free authority . . . to sail . . . to all parts, countrys and seas of the east, of the west, and of the north" he had set out to find a western route around the world to the riches, spices and perfumes of the Orient. Instead of these exotic luxuries Cabot found fish. He also found a land with an abundance of game and a generally friendly climate and within just a few years of his reports back to England the fishing peoples of Portugal, England, France and other Europeans were sailing across the Atlantic to fish the off-shore waters.

The common method of transporting fish at this time was to soak them in a brine solution in barrels. The method was, however, unsatisfactory with the barrels often splitting and the fish spoiling. Another method was chosen for the export of fish which would unwittingly alter the island's society and future. It was decided that drying the fish in the sun before returning home would ensure less spoilage and better prices. The fishermen would come ashore and build a small camp around the flakes where they laid their fish out to dry in the sun before returning to their various European ports with their catch. During the main fishing season the shores were quite busy with these camps but there was no real attempt to settle the land at this time. The three main fishing groups—the English, French and Portuguese—set up central communities at English Harbour (later Louisbourg), St. Anns Bay and Spanish Bay (Sydney) but there was no clear right of sovereignty for many years.

Around 1525 one Portuguese gentleman did claim rights to the Island for the Portuguese monarchy. He landed near Ingonish where he attempted to form a settlement. It was not a success. The settlers were totally dependant on supplies sent from Europe and these were often late or unforthcoming. The hostilities of the Indians added to their troubles and many of the settlers died from illness and starvation during the harsh winter. The settlement at Ingonish lasted less than a year.

It wasn't until the French and English began to lay serious claim to the area in the 18th century that any permanent settlement took place. In 1621 a Scotsman named Sir William Alexander received a charter for the lands that are now Nova Scotia. The following year the rights to the lands of Prince Edward Island and Cape Breton were granted to another Scot, Sir Robert Gordon. Although the numbers of immigrant families were still small, the intention was to keep the areas run in traditional Scottish manner. A series of baronices were set up to control the land and to maintain the proper feudal system of management then common to the British Isles. At that period great expanses of land were being granted or offered for purchase to the noble lords of Europe by their monarchs in return for past favors. But the lands granted offered little hope of immediate prosperity, wild and untamed as they were.

Of the groups of settlers that were to risk the hardships offered by Cape Breton over the next decades two are particularly worth mentioning, more for their stamina and endurance than their success. In 1629 Lord Ochiltree, James Stewart, bought a baronetcy for 200 livres and together with 60 trusting souls fitted out a ship and sailed for the island. He landed at Baleine in the southeast and after the preliminary work of clearing for buildings he requested tribute as a baron from the various foreign fishermen in the local waters. In so doing he upset one Captain Charles Daniel, a loyal employee of the Company of New France. Before long Daniel raided Lord Ochiltree and his settlement, made them prisoners and forced them to work building fortifications around Daniel's own encampment at St. Anns Bay before being sent back to Europe. Of the 50 people Daniel left as a garrison for the settlement many were to die from the hardships of the Cape Breton winter and the curse of scurvy.

Another unsuccessful attempt at settlement was made by one Nicholas Denys in 1632 when he arrived from France with Governor de Razilly. He sought control over much of the maritime area, then called Acadia by the French. Ousted from the mainland by other French nobles he set up posts at both St. Peters in Chetabucto Bay and St. Anns on the eastern side facing the Atlantic. Ousted once more because of power struggles he showed incredible fortitude and reestablished the settlement at St. Peters. Once again he was forced to leave by creditors who imprisoned him in Port Royal on the island of Madame. Released by the British commander Robert Sedgewick when he captured the fort in 1654, Denys returned to France where he received a commission from the King appointing him his Governor and Lieutenant-General in the countries of the Gulf, Islands of Newfoundland, Cape Breton, St. John and other adjacent islands. He settled once more in St. Peters until a disastrous fire in the 1660s forced him to leave. He returned finally to France and in 1672 wrote the first authoritative history and description of the maritime coastal lands including Cape Breton titled *"Description Geographique et historique des costes de L'Amerique septentrionale, avec l'histoire naturelle du pais."*

During the first years of discovery and settlement, the sovereignty of Cape Breton, as with much of the mainland, was in constant debate between the French and the English. Settlement was not openly encouraged but as the claimants battled for possession of Canada the populace slowly increased because of the support communities needed for the various armies landed on the shores.

In 1712, more than 200 years after Cabot first sighted land off the Cape Breton coast, the Treaty of Utrecht divided the lands between the French and English. The French lost Newfoundland, Acadia and Nova Scotia to the British but kept control of Prince Edward Island and Cape Breton. The French saw in Cape Breton the key to their presence and power on the continent. The construction of the impressive fortress at Louisbourg was the result. Initially the French brought in a few less than 200 immigrants from settlements in Newfoundland to Louisbourg and again the harshness and deprivations of the winter took their toll. Indeed, if it had not been for supplies finally sent from the French garrison at Quebec, starvation might have killed most of the settlers.

The fort designed after the style of Vauban, France's great fortification architect, became an incomparable structure on the continent. Inside the massive walls and bastions there were apartments for the governor, quarters for the officers and soldiers, an armory, chapel, hospital, shops and houses. It seems incongruous that at the very time when the immigrants were starving from lack of supplies, great shiploads of stone were brought from Europe to help fortify the walls and decorate the buildings. Although the French saw Cape Breton as the key to all of Canada, it was in many ways more than that. Through the series of events that took place during the next few decades much of the history of the continent can be linked to this particular Cape Breton fort.

Despite their great ambition the French lost Louisbourg to the New Englanders in 1745 after a long and painful seige. The British then handed the fort back to the French in 1748, a decision that understandably greatly annoyed the British colonists along the American seaboards, many of whose numbers had fought and died while taking the fort and later maintaining it for the British crown. Nearly 1000 are buried in the cemetery at Rochefort Point, the victims of privation, illness and political ambition.

Again in 1756, at a time when the Seven Years War in Europe had expanded to the colonies, the fort saw battle between the French and English. The British troops under the leadership of Lord Jeffrey Amhurst and a brigadier named James Wolfe who was destined to die at Quebec during the Battle of the Plains of Abraham, took the fort back from the French after forty-seven days of bombardment. Just two years after the taking of the fort by Amhurst, it was totally levelled by military sappers under direct orders from England's George II. That the impressive fortifications of Louisbourg are visible at all today is due entirely to the devotion of modern-day historians who have taken on the job of rebuilding and restoring it.

When the British and French colonial powers signed the Treaty of Utrecht in 1713 the lot of the Acadian people throughout the maritimes was greatly changed. Because they were direct descendants of the first French families, The British were suspicious of them. After the signing of the Treaty much of their maritime homeland was claimed by the British and the Acadians were given two choices by the British Governor. Either they could leave their homes and move to Cape Breton Island where they could live under the French flag or, they could remain on their land by revoking their heritage and swearing allegiance to the British Crown. But the Acadians loved the rocky shores, the fertile valleys and their old homes in Acadia and they would not go. They stayed firmly on the land they had cleared, albeit in British territory, yet refused to swear allegiance to the English sovereign. This impasse lasted for forty years. The British seemed content with allegiance in principle only because the Acadian communities were widely spread out and offered little obvious threat.

However, in 1753, with the mounting possibility of war breaking out between the British and the French the British became concerned about the problem of the Acadians. Would these peaceful people turn against their conquerors? Would they attack Halifax? Would they harass the forces during the fighting? Once again the Acadians were asked to pledge their allegiance to Britain and once again they refused. It was too great a threat for the Governor, Charles Lawrence, who ordered their expulsion.

The Acadians were deported in 1755 with a callousness and severity that was terrifying and shameful. Uprooted from their homes and farms, they were placed aboard ships, taken to English colonies and left in small groups in the seaports along the Atlantic coast. Families were broken up and their possessions scattered. Some escaped the round-up by travelling, as others had done forty years earlier, to Quebec and Louisiana. Others escaped to the forests and mountain areas of the interior, where they remained during the war, virtually a stateless people, trusting no one and constantly in fear for their lives.

Peace and British authority over Cape Breton came with the signing of the Treaty of

Paris in 1763. The following year it was annexed to the colony of Nova Scotia. However, back in England the Board of Trade in London, still regarded the area as little more than a land base for the fishermen and a supply of good lumber for their ship-building on the mainland.

But in 1768, at the request of the British government, Samuel Holland carried out a comprehensive survey of the island. His report described the island to a great extent as it is presented to the visitor today:

> *Nature has blessed few countries with so many advantages as this Island for the convenience and number of ports . . . the general fertility of the soil . . . the quantity of timber, the many rivers, creeks, lakes, coasts, etc. abounding with fish, the innumerable game resorting here at different seasons of the year are such inducements as with a little encouragement would invite many to become settlers . . . especially when it is considered that in raising corn, vegetables, hemp and flax in lumber, in potash, but above all in the fishery . . . the most avaracious would be satisfied and the most diffident emboldened.*

But land grants were still refused, causing concern for the settlers already there. Even the cutting of lumber for personal uses by any other than a fisherman was forbidden, under a fine of one hundred pounds. It becomes understandable why at this time the population of the island was little more than 1000 in total. The situation changed in 1784 when control of the island was given to Major Joseph DesBarres, and it was returned to the status of a separate colony. DesBarres landed at Spanish Harbour and renaming it Sydney, in honour of the Lord Sydney, then Secretary of State for the colonies, designated it as the capital of Cape Breton. Although debate over land ownership was to continue on into the 1820s when the colony was re-annexed to Nova Scotia, settlement began to increase considerably.

Many of the first families to set up communities were the Acadians returning from their exiles, most settling along the western shore route of the Cabot Trail. Here they could fish the bountiful waters of the Gulf of St. Lawrence and the North Atlantic. Here also were coastal lowlands and valleys which offered a fair agriculture. Within a few short years the small groupings of houses began to grow into prospering villages.

The Acadians were farmers as well as fishermen. However, fishing remained the main industry together with some lumbering, and farming was done mainly for private sustenance. Forming tightly knit, homogenous groups, insulated from the outside by their justifiable mistrust, they determined to keep and strengthen their own traditions. They were strong believers in the Catholic church and the family unit. They were also a gay people. Dancing and partying to the Acadian fiddle and reels were, and still are, a popular way of shortening the winter months. Modern communities such as Grand Etang, Cheticamp, Belle Cote and Margaree show this pattern to this day. Most families living here live much as their ancestors did. During the summer months they have two jobs, fishing and farming, along with jobs involved with the new industry of tourism. During the winter months they repair the tools of labour and prepare for the spring.

Perhaps the most notable of the Acadian communities today is Cheticamp, with roots going all the way back to the early part of the 17th century, when it was used as a base for French fishermen. In 1790 it was a group of Acadian refugees returning from the French islands of St. Pierre and Miquelon that laid the real roots of the present-day community. With excellent fishing in the Gulf of St. Lawrence, a natural harbour that was deep and protected from the Gulf's storms, large stands of mixed timber and the lowlands before the mountains offering good farming, it soon became the centre of activity on the western side of the Island.

The families of the district - the Aucoins, d'Entrements, Boudreaux, Doucets, Lejeunes, Corniers, Bourgeois, Bernards, and Arsenaults are all descendants of the first exiled settlers. As a people they did not wish to be absorbed by either the British or French culture. They have instead maintained their own identity, a unique culture, with its own language and traditions, a heritage in which they rightly show great pride.

While the western shores were being settled by the Acadians, the eastern coves were also being claimed by the Scots, a people with an equal pride in their heritage. In 1774 the population of Cape Breton had been 1,012 with not a dozen Scots among them. By 1815 there were 6,000 Scots on the Island and by 1838 the population had jumped to 35,420 Scots living in flourishing settlements along the western coast at St. Anns Bay and around the shores of the Bras d'or Lakes. The Scots saw in the island's craggy shoreline a similarity to the Scottish highlands, from which the majority of them had emmigrated. The main communities congregated around Ingonish Beach, where sheltered by Cape Smokey and Middle Head, the promontory that divides the bay, the fishing industry thrived.

Like the Acadians, the Scots descendants of those early settlers have managed to retain many of the early traditions and the Gaelic language is still spoken in parts of Cape Breton in the original 18th century dialect.

It was of course easier for the Acadians and Scots to keep their language and customs intact on Cape Breton Island than it would have been in other parts of Canada. Isolated from the rest of Canada, the island peoples tended to be insular and the terrain of the island prevented much outside communication. In fact, there was little socialization between the island villages due to the harsh winter climate and the ruggedness of the landscape.

The building of the Cabot Trail in 1932 brought many changes to the island. Used mainly as a convoy route for the trucks which brought supplies into the villages and took out the lumber, fish and farm products, the Trail became a scenic tourist route after it was paved in 1957. The world began to intrude on the Islanders and tourism with its attendant service industries became an important part of the island's economy at a time when the profits from fishing, lumbering and mining were declining.

There has been some apprehension that the Islanders' heritage would get lost among the souvenirs on the roadside stands. But the opposite has proven true. There has been a resurgence of pride among the Cape Breton people in their traditions, their history, their very differences. There is a genuine interest in the preservation of the Gaelic and French languages, the crafts and skills of the past. Care and concern are shown about the way the area is presented to the tourists. The people of the Island are aware of the beauty surrounding them. They are proud of it. It is their heritage and because of the Cabot Trail that beauty and heritage can be enjoyed by all who travel it.

Mr. Murphy

I've lived in this area all of my life. I moved to this old house in 1924. Got married and moved in. I was born about two miles from here. We had our 50th wedding anniversary here two years ago and all the family was here—our children, the grandchildren and the great grandchildren. There's 52 grandchildren and 14 great grandchildren. Oh yes, we were happy, we've had a good life you know.

There's quite a few of the children still live around here. They're all mostly here on Cape Breton Isle except there's one moved to Vancouver and a girl in Massachusetts. I go up there every so often. She plays the fiddle for the old folks home up there and she wants me to go and play with her. I play the fiddle and sometimes the mandolin. But I'm not what you'd call — a musician you know, I never could afford to study music but I've been playing for as long as I can remember.

Now, I had a small farm and the mill. Kept a few cows, just enough for the milk and butter—just farmed more or less for ourselves. You had to at that time you know, grow your own food and that. It wasn't what you'd call good farming really. How could you farm, how could you compete with the farms in the west there in the prairies where they don't have to put fertilizer and manure or anything on the land, don't have to pick up stones or pull stumps? You couldn't farm more than 30 acres here—you had enough for yourself, for your own use. Oh, it was a pretty good life if you worked at it. Some need a whistle to get up in the morning but you had to be your own whistle and get up early to do the chores.

Do you know that in this district there used to be, oh, I think, 15 saw mills at one time? This is back 30 years or more I reckon. Yes, there were that many and they were all busy then. Now there's only the one that's still in use and I hear—now, I don't know for sure—but I heard that they're finding things a bit slow and might close up. Well, that would be the end of the logging around here then. I remember when nearly every family roundabouts had a man working in the mills or up in the woods cutting timber.

There are roads you know, old logging trails around here that go maybe 40 miles into the woods. Well, I tell you, that was something in the old days when you used to take a team of horses in there in the winter to skid the logs out. It was so deep, the snow, that often you had a time getting the horses to walk, it was so deep. And cold, oh boy.

We used to cut pit props for the coal companies, six feet long and they couldn't be under three inches at the top nor over six inches at the bottom. We used to get six dollars a cord at the side of the road for them. Can you imagine, I cut 60 cords one summer? I couldn't say for sure but they'd maybe get thirty, forty dollars a cord for them now, you know. It's changed a good deal. But there's not the logs being cut now—just some pulp wood I guess—there's not the interest in lumbering there used to be.

We had the mill right around the corner there a bit—right where the Trail is now. Well it must have been, oh, I don't rightly remember just when it was, but when they were putting the road through and I sold it. Yes I got a hundred and twenty-five dollars for it. I don't know now but then it seemed not too bad a price. But I should have said "no you move the mill and set it up down the ways a bit." That was the big mistake I made I reckon.

Take what's happening on the Trail now around the island with these tourists—it's good. Brings money into the community you know. Everybody gets a little of it. Now that's my feeling on it. Some say they don't like it but I think it's good. It's a friendly place you know. We treat everybody the same as though they're a friend or visitor. I mean for anyone to think they're better than anyone else, I call that stupid because they're not, you know. You could be me and I could be you.

It was never what you'd call a lonely existence—not as lonely as it is now. Those days

everybody was friends but the television and the radio spoiled all that. You used to go out, play cards or visiting most every night, going from one house to another. Now, you're not wanting to go in case someone's watching some television film.

We were the first here abouts to get the television but now most have one, I reckon. But the television, that was a big mistake they made. They should have had that two nights a week from six o'clock until nine or ten and that should have been it and then they would have looked forward to watch it like a night out. They should have done that all over the world and then it wouldn't have changed the ways so much.

Joe Delaney

I guess I've lived here pretty well all my life. In 1922 my mother and father moved to the States and we lived there for ten years. We came back in 1932 and ever since I've resided here.

I've never really been a fisherman here, you know. I did a little bit of farming and labouring on the Trail when it was being built. In the fall sometimes I'd try to get a place on one of the boats to do the mackeral fishing. We all used to try to get onto a boat because in the short period of time that the mackeral were being caught you could make good money compared to what you'd likely make working on the farm or whatever. That was during the war and the year I recall was the best year of mackeral fishing was in 1944 and they were paying 14 cents a pound.

One day I remember we went out—there was eight of us on the boat, everybody sharing like equal—didn't matter if you caught 500 fish more than the other guy everybody got the same share at the end of the day. And we took enough mackeral for each man to get $1404. Now just a minute, no, the decimal point's in the wrong place—yes, it was a $140.00 to a man. Now that was a lot of money for a man in those times, a lot of money. Before that you'd get, six cents, maybe seven cents a pound for mackeral. Then it went back down you know. Today I suppose they get around nine, ten cents a pound. It's too bad the weather's so bad this fall because the mackeral are there but the boats can't get out—it's too windy, the sea's too rough. But if they could get out they'd make good money this year.

You have to go out every day when you know where the mackeral's at. Now they go out with the draggers and they catch a lot but quite a few still go out with the hand line. They have what you'd call sort of a jig at the end of the line and if you get a good lot, well maybe you'd have two lines working. If the mackeral's scarce you'd maybe have four lines out that you'd work. But once the mackeral strike you'd better haul in those other two lines or otherwise they are all going to get tangled in to one another and then you're in a heck of a mess.

The bigger boats, well my god, they're well-rigged today compared to back in the depression. My god, what they had then was twenty-two footers and then in '39 when the war broke out the fishermen started to get bigger boats. They got the forty-footers and in those bigger boats eight could go out so there was a captain and seven others. Well, like I said, everybody shared and the boat shared also. Like he got one-eighth, so the captain and the boat were doing pretty good.

For a while there weren't too many young people wanting to get into fishing but in a couple of years I think you're going to see more of the young class going into it. We have some young men out there that went into fishing because their father is fishing and they went with their father. And those guys out there fishing are making a good living now, doing just as good as anyone working on construction or with pulp wood or any other occupation around here. Those guys are fishing year round during the season, and during the winter spell when there's ice and no fishing—well, then they get

unemployment insurance.

Besides, when the pulp wood industry first started you could get contracts of, let's say, a hundred thousand cords and today it's cut down to fifty-five, sixty thousand cords. We notice that the work is less and the men get laid off sooner. Thank god they can make their stamps for unemployment insurance. If it wasn't for that we'd be in trouble down here, that's for sure.

Now when the Cabot Trail was built that made a difference, oh yes, did it ever. It's one of the main industries, you might as well say, of this area. Now we have the fishing, the lumbering, the pulp and logging like, and then the tourists. If it wasn't for the tourism there would be quite a few out of work, let's put it that way. Because you take the hotels and cabins all around the Trail—they are employing a lot of people.

Now you take for instance the people in the handicrafts—my wife herself, she makes mats, you know, and it's these tourists who buy them. The women make not just mats but these four-inch and eight-inch squares with a picture of a lobster on it and they go like butter in the sun, they can't make enough of them. They are doing good, the crafts down in this area. Now this hook work I'm talking about, well that's been going on from 1800.

Like I was saying, the Cabot Trail created not only wonders for every family but for the area as a whole. It also made a big change for the people here themselves—they got to know one another more. By having this Trail it's easier to visit—the young people are mixing more. Now for the older people it hasn't made much of a difference perhaps. But the younger people, they mix in at the school level and with the hockey games and that—one village playing another. They go into Sydney in just a couple of hours drive. That's how they get acquainted and that's good, oh yes, is it ever.

I worked on the Trail right up there to MacKenzie mountain. That was hard up there. You have the French mountain first and then a stretch on top and then MacKenzie. It was unbelievable, the blasting and the jack-hammering, the work that was done there. It was mostly built by people around here, around the Trail in the different communities. They brought in some of the key men, engineers and that but as far as 90 per cent of the work, it was the local men who built it.

Cheticamp Boatman

We still have this very strong close-knit family feeling here, but I think that is not very different from any small village you know. Perhaps it is strongest here being an island and that. We're more separated from the outside world.

The young people they tend to marry their friends locally quite a bit. It is not necessarily the thing to do but if they don't go anywhere else, if they don't go to the cities, well, they don't have much of a choice.

I lived in Toronto for fourteen years and all the time I was broke and now I've been back here for two years and I am still broke so what does that mean? What's the difference? But I like it here more than in the city so that's why I stay I guess.

This used to be a ship-building yard at one time but not any more. We still do some little repairs to boats but mostly we sell finished building materials for houses and that. We don't really have the time now to work repairing the boats. We work making cabinets and that. That doesn't leave us too much time to work on the boats.

It's getting really busy down here now. In the last couple of years in a little place like this they have put up fifty, maybe sixty new houses. For a small place like this that is tremendous. Five years before that it was something to see five new houses built in a year. Now it's thirty-five, forty new ones.

It's mostly, I would say that about fifty per cent of the people who are building up here are people who were living in Toronto, Montreal or down in the States, Boston. Originally from hereabouts they had moved down there

looking for work and now they have come back. Everyone seems to be coming back, in the last couple of years it seems to be the trend, leaving the city coming back to their old homes in the country.

Fish is expensive today. Even down here you can pay two dollars a pound. It used to be down here a salmon, a five-pound salmon you'd sell it for a quarter or fifty cents. This was when I was a kid, I remember that if all you wanted was cod or mackeral they'd give it you. Now the fishermen get thirty, forty cents a pound for haddock. But it's good that it has changed. Before the future really didn't have much for anyone down here. You can't have a community where no one can afford to spend anything. Some of the changes have not been so good I suppose. It depends how you look at things. A lot of the old ways, the traditions have had to change because they were old-fashioned and that's a pity I guess, but not too many were lost. And now the government is building an Acadian village to promote the traditions. That's important because down here a lot of the income that we get is from tourism. The tourism and fishing are about what keeps the island alive really I guess. I don't mind myself, some of the old people they get a bit fed up with the visitors sometimes but they don't really mind.

People are generally proud of being Acadian you know. Of course not everyone cares. There are some people who want to keep the French strong here but it's very difficult you know. You have Pleasant Bay up the road a bit where it's Scot and down in Margaree as well and I wouldn't like to see the people not getting along because of language. In the schools they are bringing back the French language. Not so much to speak French but to keep some of the old ways, the heritage alive so they know what it used to be like. When I went to school it wasn't like that—it was all in English but now they teach arithmetic in French.

Cheticamp store proprietor

Now I had this store built in 1935. It was a good job, it's still here, and good and strong still. When it was first built the shop was three feet above the road—there was steps up and it was seven feet from the road. Now it's right on the roadside and there are two steps down to the doorway. That shows the changes made to the roads. I had the warehouse over the way there and we used to back a three-ton truck with supplies up to it. You can't park a wheelbarrow there now, the road's that wide. Of course there weren't many people who had cars in those days. The Trail then was just dirt mostly, just a wagon track in parts.

This was in the days of rum smuggling. It was good rum, St. Pierre rum from the French islands of St. Pierre and Miquelon. The schooners would go there and load up and they'd come in about three miles off shore and you'd see a light. Well, on a calm night anything that could float or be rowed went out. While you were aboard the rum was free, you could drink all you wanted and then you'd buy what you wanted and row it back to shore and that's when the games started. The sherriffs who patrolled along here would try to find out where the rum was being landed. So everybody had different kinds of gimmicks or tricks to hide it, you see. One famous one was to tie your case with a rope and a buoy to the other end of the rope with a bag of salt. You'd drop it into the ocean and the water would melt the salt and after a week say, the buoy would come to the surface and you'd

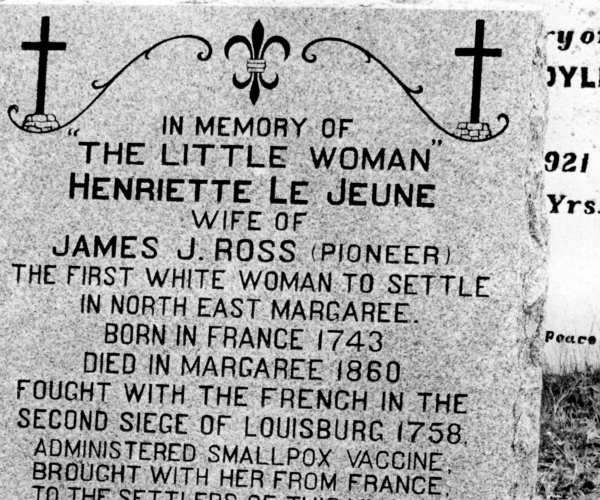

IN MEMORY OF
"THE LITTLE WOMAN"
HENRIETTE Le JEUNE
WIFE OF
JAMES J. ROSS (PIONEER)
THE FIRST WHITE WOMAN TO SETTLE
IN NORTH EAST MARGAREE.
BORN IN FRANCE 1743
DIED IN MARGAREE 1860
FOUGHT WITH THE FRENCH IN THE
SECOND SIEGE OF LOUISBURG 1758.
ADMINISTERED SMALLPOX VACCINE,
BROUGHT WITH HER FROM FRANCE,
TO THE SETTLERS OF THIS VALLEY.
BENEFACTRESS OF ALL BOTH WHITE
AND INDIAN.
ERECTED BY HER GREAT GRANDSON
THOMAS E. ROSS

ry of
OYLE

921
Yrs.

Peace

just row out and haul up your rum. Or another way was to put it at the bottom just off the shore and then cut holes in the ice in the winter and get it that way. Oh, there were many tricks, you know.

It used to be really isolated here in those days of course. You depended a good deal on supplies like flour, molasses and pork. These were the main things for the winter. The people were poor here. They had potatoes they grew themselves and a few had a pig or two. For the winter each family had to buy enough to last them through to the spring when the ice would melt and the boats could get in again. I've seen many a fall when there have been 5000 bags of flour stored up for the winter. And in Cap Rouge people would come down in the winter with dogsleds to buy flour and goods for the winter.

There's something interesting about some of the houses here. One of our bad points here is our southeast wind. It's a very vicious wind. The cause of it is that on the south side of the mountains, which is generally the warmer side, you get a southerly or southeast wind. It hits the mountains and has to climb up and it cools and then travels along the tops, the plateau and then when it comes to this side it rushes down—and oh boy, can it get strong. It causes a lot of damage. We've had winds here of 140 miles an hour. Really bad. Well, you can't go out in that sort of wind. So a lot of the farmhouses here have the barn built right onto the house. Now this lets the farmer feed his cattle or pigs without going out, 'cause the wind would rip the door frame right off easy as anything. Some houses have cables to hold them down and some have gravel put into the walls.

The people round here. they fear the wind. If there is any chance of it coming up they won't got out in the boats fishing at all and if they are out they just pull in the nets and come right in.

In the old days all the fishing was done in small boats by trawling or hand fishing. Some of the fishing was good then. But now the fish are scarce and the fish themselves have changed. It's been fished out you see.

Why, it used to be nothing for a fisherman to go out and get a 1000 lbs. of haddock—now you're lucky to get one. Cod is the same thing. Fished out. It's these big boats you see. They net in maybe 10,000 lbs. of fish in one catch and they throw perhaps three-quarters of that back into the sea as dead fish; it's too small or the wrong type for what they want. They only keep the bigger fish so they're destroying an awful lot of fish just to catch some. Now with the trawl fishing that didn't happen because it would always be the bigger fish that would go after the bait and the smaller ones would have a chance to grow.

There are three or four basic types of fishing—there's the drag which drags along the bottom behind these big boats and picks up everything in sight, the trawl with the baited hook, the net and the hand line.

Spring is for lobster, and dragging for sole and codfish. The summer months are generally slow because the fish are too far out and move up the Gulf of St. Lawrence. Around Christmas is when the freezeup starts and the Gulf waters here freeze solid. Then in the spring it's the breakup and the fishermen are all waiting for it to happen because immediately after the ice does break up they want to get out and set their lobster traps, you see. Now, some years it plays tricks on them—there have been times when the ice will move out just a few miles and the season could be on and they have to gamble because if they set their traps out there and the wind shifts overnight it can bring the ice back in and wipe out their traps. Some years men have lost every trap they put out in one night, terrible it is. So around breakup time the tension down here gets pretty bad.

The first three days are very critical because the traps are still dry, they haven't soaked up with water to get weight in them and they move around easy and get broken on the rocks. And it costs eight to ten dollars to make a trap and some of them have 200 traps out there. Mind you, some of those fishermen, in a good year with the lobsters can make a tidy living.

The Trail

I think of Cape Breton as a lonely child in the family of Canada. Although part of Nova Scotia, it is defiantly an island, separated from the mainland Canada by the narrow Canso Strait, a little less than a mile wide. When the causeway was completed one old lady is supposed to have said during her family's dinner-time prayers: "And thank God for having at last made Canada a part of Cape Breton."

Baddeck, a quiet, somewhat sleepy village on the Trans-Canada highway, is considered by most to be the beginning and end of the Cabot Trail, although purists say there is no real start or finish. One of the most prosperous villages on the island, Baddeck lives largely on tourism and there are many motels with lawn chairs hospitably set out so that visitors may sit and look out over the water. The town also has shops, banks, a library, hospital and government buildings and at lunch schoolchildren, many of them bussed into Baddeck from outlying districts, sit and giggle in the Chinese restaurant. As they play tag, throw frisbees and flirt on the street outside, their Indian, French, Scottish and English heritage is reflected in their countenances.

Alexander Graham Bell made Baddeck his summer home and it is easy to see why. The vista presented to him from Red Point—the lakes with their gently sloping green banks, the small fishing boats in the beautiful natural harbour—so entranced Bell that he soon acquired property after his first visit in 1886. Infatuated with the potential of flight, Bell conducted many experiments with kites in Baddeck. The townsfolk were not impressed. "Fooling away the whole blessed day flying kites . . . it's the greatest foolishness I ever did see," a Baddeck boatman remarked. But Bell's "foolishness" led to the first recorded flight in the British Empire when in 1908 he and his colleagues installed an engine in a kite.

The Alexander Graham Bell museum in Baddeck, architecturally resembling his tetrahedron kites, is a major tourist attraction. But then, Baddeck has always been popular with tourists and in the late 1800s merchants and families of good standing discovered the beauty of the area. Their summer homes, many of them large and impressively situated along the sloping hills, are still standing. Baddeck was also the centre for a prosperous ship-building industry with a bustling harbour. The old homes and warehouses along the harbour are basically unchanged; neat, freshly painted they reflect the pride felt by the citizens for their town.

The freshly painted red mailbox at the side of the road made me stop the car. It seemed to me symbolic of the changes the island's society had gone through in the years since the completion of the Cabot Trail. Before the roadway, the mail, newspapers, indeed, any report from the world outside, had to come by way of the supply ships or by the hardy traveller. In winter when the sea froze over and the snow made journeys through the wooded tracks dangerous, if not impossible, news was slow to reack this part of Canada. Today the islanders are well aware of the outside world. They watch the eleven-o'clock news on television, listen to the radio and read the daily papers. But none of this has changed the pride the islanders still take in their independence nor the love they feel for their solitary way of life. The fresh paint on the mailbox and the bright yellow siding of the house behind are not done for the tourists' sake but for the pleasure they themselves take in their homes and land.

Piles of logs neatly stacked along the roadways are everywhere, awaiting shipment to the pulp and paper industry. To the small woodlot owner and the farmer with a stand of trees, his trees are his "bank" to be spent if the need arises. But many piles of logs rotting at the side of the road are evidence that the industry is in a state of decline.

Everywhere there seemed to be yellow school buses. Driving the Trail when the school day was over was much like following a convoy, which stopped constantly to drop off the island's future. Bussed to a worldly education each day, the children return each night to the family stronghold with its security and traditions.

Like any island fishing community, death has always been a way of life on Cape Breton Island. The small cemetery at Goose Cove, on a hill overlooking the harbour of St. Anns, is typical of many on the island. The Scottish names on the gravestones—MacDonald, MacKenzie, Murdoch, MacLeod, MacLennan, MacRitchie, MacAulay, MacAskill, etc.—and the epitaphs which so often simply say "Lost at sea" tell the island's story—a story, like the environment, which remains constant.

As you drive along the Trail you will see many small farms situated close to the sea. Although fishing and lumbering were the important industries, the family farm was always considered the islanders' larder. But the small Cape Breton farm has little place in the world of agrobusiness today. Old barns, weathered and leaning, exhausted by their battles with the island winters, are a common sight. The land here was never rich enough for good crops and when the farmer gives up and finally leaves, the land's return to the natural wild covering is rapid. The first sapplings encroach upon the ploughed fields within a few seasons.

Passing through the woodland, along the shore, the feeling of expectation heightens. Every corner turned along the Trail brings a new experience.

Sometimes you will drive past small neat villages, other times past a group of scattered buildings with a church, perhaps a shop or two. Between these communities are the farms of the islanders, some of the fields worked, some run over with forest. Chickens cluck under overhanging trees, joyously playing with the sun.

Looking back along Wreck Cove one sees a land that has changed little since the days when the Micmac Indians hunted the bountiful game of the woods and waters.

Mr. Morrison of Wreck Cove:

We were one of the original families here—I don't know just when, but long before my time. Yes, the Morrisons, the McClouds and McDermitts are just about the oldest names around this part.

"When the Trail was paved back in the fifties it made a tremendous change you know. Before that if you had a car it would be about a day's journey to drive to Sydney. Now it takes maybe an hour. In the winter you couldn't travel anywhere really, before the Trail. It was remote, I guess you'd say. At one time all the communities would have to get all their supplies in the fall of the year and they'd have to last till spring. That's when they used to get their supplies by boat. The freeze-up usually comes just before Christmas and you couldn't go out in a boat then. When the bad weather started you couldn't insure your boat if you did try to make it out, it was that bad at times.

"Talking about being remote, my family used to own a warehouse and there was one year when they had the mail stuck in there for three months. The snows were so bad we couldn't even get it to Ingonish. Smokey mountain was blocked all winter, couldn't get no horse across, couldn't even walk there. This was long before the roads were kept open. Now of course the roads are kept open all along the Trail. There's none of the remoteness now."

After the leisurely peacefulness of the Trail which has so far taken one past small villages and tranquil farmlands, Cape Smokey seems to rise ahead of the traveller like some prehistoric being. This feeling is intensified by the scarred barren surface of the mountain, created by a fire which ravaged its thickly treed surface in the sixties. The mountain drops sheer to the sea, its feet washed by the Atlantic, its summit often shrouded in morning mists from which it derives its name—Smokey. In little more than a mile the road gradiant climbs 1,200 feet and when you are nearing the top you can see that the forest is beginning to come back. The old trees, still standing defiant of the wind and weather, give refuge to the young shrubs and weeds that will form the new forest. The burnt-over areas reseed naturally—first comes the aptly-named fireweed, followed by biennials and perennials such as bristly aralia, blueberries and raspberries, then comes aspens, wild cherries and birches. These are mostly weed trees which provide cover for the seedlings of spruce and fir and in time these conifers form a new forest replacing the one burnt over. To see this mantle of new green life spreading over the mountain reassures one, once again, about the healing power of nature.

Coming down the northern side of Cape Smokey I began to see the type of Cape Breton fishing villages I had pictured in my mind's eye but had not yet actually seen. Baddeck, though in a rural location, still had all the urban trappings of a town, which it indeed was. And although charming, the dozen or so communities I had passed while driving along the eastern shore, the scattered groupings of homes and small farms in close proximity, had not lived up to my private image of a fishing village which was, I suppose, reminiscent of the villages I had known along the Atlantic seaboard of the British Isles.

But when the road crossed Cape Smokey and the villages of Ingonish came into view I knew that I had found what I had been searching for. Nestled along the shore of Ingonish Bay, split into south and north sections by the promontory called Middle Head, are villages in which the visitor will find lobster pots stacked along the quays, weather-bronzed menfolk spreading nets out to dry in the noonday sun and white-aproned housewives.

First there is Ingonish Ferry, a small village made all the more sleepy by the fact that the paving of the Trail has made the ferry largely unnecessary. The road dips down to sea level as it crosses the marshy mouth of the Ingonish River at South Ingonish Harbour where lobster men tie up their boats and sport-fishing trips can be organized in the summer months. Ingonish Beach is the actual town and is also the entrance to the Cape Breton Highlands National Park. Then there is Ingonish Centre, my private image of a fishing village come to life. The roadway curves gently along the shore of the North Bay and the Atlantic waters lapping the stretches of sand seemed tamed here. The homes, spread out at ease along the Trail and back inland a small way, are cheerful with painted clapboard reflecting the morning sun and gardens with flowers and vegetables.

The traditional business of the village is still fishing but that has changed considerably over the past couple of decades. The catches have become smaller and the individual fisherman has little chance of making a living as the bigger commercial fishing boats now go out for days at a time. The sport fishing for which Ingonish was once renowned has also fallen in popularity. During the thirties and forties, Ingonish offered summer visitors some of the best sword fishing in the world but as the waters became fished out and regulations were put into effect, the sport dropped off.

As with much of the eastern and northern sections of the Trail, the heritage of the Ingonish communities is largely Scots. It was also one of the earliest places settled on the island and one of the first camp sites set up by the early European visitors who fished the coastal waters and then came ashore to dry their catch before the long journey to their home ports. The first settlement was around 1525 when Jose Alvare Fagundes, with the help of a grant from the Portuguese throne, brought a small band of people to Ingonish. But the winter hardships and hositilities from the Indian natives proved too difficult for the settlers and the site was abandoned. When in the late 1700s large numbers of Scots immigrated to Cape Breton, Ingonish was chosen as a settlement. They found a land where the softly rolling slopes of the mountainous interior of the island offered not only good game but protection from the elements on three sides of the bay and with waters teeming with fish which would provide their daily sustenance.

The pride the people of Ingonish feel in their Scots heritage is very evident. The

Gaelic language, although not used by everyone as French is in the western-shore Acadian communities, can still be heard in the towns and villages. Indeed, there has been a surge of interest and more use of the Gaelic language in the last decade. It is not really surprising that the Scottish heritage has withstood the changing years in Ingonish. Until the paving of the Cabot Trail in the 1930s, Ingonish was totally isolated from the outside world except by travel over the sea. The Canadian English spoken here is so broadly accented that the visitor may feel he has travelled to a village in Scotland.

I t is a half hour before the first light of a new day. The leaves on the trees along the shore, the grass along the footpath, the stones on the silent shore are all covered with an early frost. Then the birds begin to rustle in the trees, the sky changes to a blue haze and the clouds appearing from the mists of dawn begin to reflect the warmth which will come. As the sun breaks free of the horizon the sound of a new day begins. The birds sing, the grass waves gently in the first rays of the sun, the frost on the leaves turns to dew and slowly drips to the earth. The balance between nature and daybreak seemed suddenly audible. The new day had arrived.

Although Neil's Harbour is not actually on the Cabot Trail, the half mile deviation to visit it is well worthwhile. Here is a Cape Breton fishing village that appears, on the surface at least, to have changed very little over the years. The small houses nestled together on the hill overlooking the natural harbour present an image which is quaint, peaceful – ideal for a picture postcard. But Neil's Harbour is far more than just a picturesque community – it is a working one as well. The rows of old weather-beaten fishermen's huts, storing all the tools of their trade, are a hive of energy in the early morning when the boats are made ready to go out to sea. There is also a fish processing plant kept busy with the catches brought in each day.

The old man was sitting in front of a barrow of cod that had just been brought in. He was cleaning and salting the fish for himself. He remembered the old days when he used to go out himself. Fishing was a lot better in those days he said. But then, life was a lot different in those days also. There was no government help – if you didn't work you went hungry. Mind you, it was maybe a bit better in some ways for the old people at that time. Then the fish were given to the old ones, but now he had to buy it. He missed the sea. Sometimes he went out by himself for a morning to see if he could still handle the jigger the way he used to. He didn't go out much, though. He nearly drowned a few years back when an Atlantic storm sunk his boat from under him and he was in the water nearly three hours before he was rescued.

From Neil's Harbour the Trail turns abruptly inland crossing the northern plateau. Once you have left behind the rock-pounding power of the Atlantic waters the land takes on a more tranquil appearance. This is the northern section of the National park. The forests line the roadway, as it meanders along up and down small hills heading for the communities of South Harbour and Cape North, in the shadow of the Aspy mountain that dissects the finger of the island. Here in the valleys, where the silt of the rivers has provided a fair soil, farming is more important. Cattle graze in the fields and small groups of farm buildings dot the landscape. From Cape North the mountainous terrain of Cape Breton becomes immediately apparent. Out of the trees rises North Mountain, an ominous looking body of rock that is a real barrier not only between the geography of the east and west coasts but also between the Celtic and Acadian bloodlines of the inhabitants.

The Trail looks fragile as it weaves upward like a silk thread along the very edge of the rock. Wisps of smoke from logging camps form a haze that makes the colours almost monotone at a distance. Cut from the very edge of the mountain the road zig-zags upwards around perilous corners that overlook the forests below, and offers a view as magnificent as any traveller could wish for. At the top, the trees stand sentry as if guarding the island against unknown fears.

The first time I drove around the Cabot Trail it was spring and the forest slopes from the mountain valleys were covered in the soft green of the new season. It was beautiful and soothing and it was not until I travelled across the MacKenzie and French mountains that the real might of this wild, unaltered land affected me. Up here on the wild mountain plateaus the environment takes on a cold, almost brutal atmosphere and it was this section across the island's mountain spine that was most difficult for the road engineers to complete. It is a tundra-like land with countless bogs and lakes turned black by the peat covering. The trees are stunted and gnarled by the winds blowing constantly across the open plateaus. In winter the temperature plummets and snows rage across in terrifying blizzards. The roadway is kept clear at all times but the emergency survival huts along the route show that danger is very real in this area. Once again one finds oneself marvelling that the early settlers managed to make this island home.

But if the mountain terrain is harsh, it is also impressive and impossible to ignore. The mountains demand your attention. And if you stand at the side of the road and look out over the valleys far below with streams rushing down to the sea, the setting sun bright in the late evening sky shimmering on silvered waters, the question of the settlers' choice seems easier to understand. The pure, unspoiled beauty of the region is the answer.

In 1947 a terrifying fire destroyed more than seven thousand acres of prime forest land along the mountain slopes of the Grand Anse valley. For fifteen days the fire raged toward the village of Pleasant Bay, driven onward by strong winds blowing down the mountain slopes. There seemed no hope for the community as the flames closed in on all sides and many people left their homes. Prayer seemed the only recourse, the only defence. On the fifteenth day the winds suddenly dropped and then changed direction. The fire's route was turned back and it burnt itself out on its own ashes.

The memory of the devastation is easily recalled by the local people a generation later and the scars on the mountains can be seen by the visitor from promontories high atop Mount MacKenzie. But the strength and determination of nature can also be seen—the slopes that were so badly scorched are now thirty years later, covered again in green growth.

After MacKenzie Mountain comes French Mountain and then the island barrier is passed. Slowly the Trail makes its way back towards the sea. It is this area around Cap Rouge on the shores of the Gulf of St. Lawrence that offers the best-known vistas of Cape Breton. Here the roadway hugs itself to the mountainside down to the water's edge and up over rock out-crops. It is along here that one of the best views of the island's rock formations is to be had. As the weather, winds and storms have eaten away at the land's surface many examples of the island's structure have been uncovered.

Perhaps the most interesting aspect of the Cabot Trail is the differing landscapes and social environments it offers on such a comparatively short journey. Nowhere is this more obvious than when the Trail descends from the mountainous spine toward the flatlands of the western coast. This now is the Acadian Centre of the Cabot Trail and it has a character and heritage very much its own. Here the landscape takes on a completely new appearance. The mountains become a distant vast backdrop separated from the waters of the Gulf of St. Lawrence by a wide, gently undulating plateau of small valleys and patchwork fields. But it is the change in habitation which is most noticeable. Where the highland areas, though impressive and exciting to travel across, had offered little opportunity for even the most courageous homesteading, the roadway now hugging the plateau's edge runs through a series of small villages. And where the eastern side of the island had been Gaelic in origin, on the western coast the names of the villages reflect the Acadian heritage: Petit Etang, Cheticamp, Terre Noire and Belle Cote. Rising over the small clap-board buildings of Cheticamp is the impressive spire of the Roman Catholic church, a testimony in stone to the religious beliefs of the Acadians. In fact, it is in Cheticamp that the Acadian tradition in Canada is considered by historians and sociologists to be best preserved.

That the Acadian communities along the western section of the Trail are so distinctive is due very much to the history of the people themselves. Their lineage dates back to the early 1600s when a small group of French Huguenots settled on the island in Passamaquoddy Bay and a year later moved to Port Royal. The maritime area of Canada they settled in was called *Acadie* (In English, Acadia) and the settlers, Acadians.

From the very beginning the Acadians faced serious obstacles. They were raided by English colonists from the south and they became embroiled in the conflicting interests of England and France. Theirs was not to be a life destined for much ease or happiness. The first settlement at Port Royal was dispersed by a raiding force from Virginia in 1613 and eight years later their lands were granted by James VI of Scotland to Sir William Alexander and his heirs and named Nova Scotia. The lands later changed hands between the French and English until in 1670 the colony was given back to France. For the following forty years the settlements prospered and the population rose. But by the end of the century the British and French began fighting in earnest for the rights to the land. With the signing of the Treaty of Utrecht in 1713 Nova Scotia was given to the British and Cape Breton ceded to France. The Acadians were given two choices by the British: They could either move to French territories or stay in Nova Scotia as British crown subjects. But the Acadians did not consider themselves affiliated with either flag. They were Acadians.

For the fifty years that the British and French monarchies continued their struggle in Canada, the Acadians lived a precarious existence. A number of attempts were made to persuade them to take the oath of allegiance to the British crown or to move to Cape Breton but as the Acadians stubbornly refused there were no real attempts made to force them in the matter. But they were distrusted by both British and French and treated as nuisances and pawns.

A new and terrible era began for the Acadians in 1753 when Charles Lawrence became Governor of Nova Scotia and determined to put up with them no longer. Under his rule they were forcibly expelled from their native lands with a callous persecution which did not end until the signing of the Treaty of Paris in 1763 when France relinquished claims to North American territory.

By this time the Acadians had become a resilient and independent people. They formed insular and proud communities where they practised their Roman Catholic faith, caring little what went on outside their villages. These are traits that remain with them to this day, often to their advantage and sometimes, to their disadvantage.

One of the better descriptions of the Acadian people is by the Acadian scholar Father Anselme Chaisson:

> *The Acadian carries in his soul the traces of past sufferings. His ancestors lived for a long time dispossessed, hunted down and dishonoured. The earliest pages of his history were written in his blood; he still carries the mark. Brutally uprooted from his land he has now turned to the sea . . . For a long period in their history, the Acadians lived in isolation. On the whole this has tended to hold back their development and to make them feel inferior . . . Having suffered, the Acadian is kind to others, understanding, sympathetic, sensitive, compassionate and hospitable.*

Driving southerly on the western shore of the Trail, one passes along the plateau edge where rugged cliffs drop sharply to the water with its terrifying undercurrents. Here and there, small harbours are reached down dusty tracks. They might consist of no more than a few sheds and a small quay used by a couple of fishermen who today fish only the short lobster season in the spring.

To the left of the Trail, in the mile or so that the plateau stretches to the mountains, the land is dotted with farms. The farming has never been rich here, the soil more suitable for forest covering than crops. In fact, farming is a very small part of the local economy and although you can see tractors working the land and cattle grazing, the potatoes and vegetables are generally planted for home use and are not for sale. The land looks sleepy, as though resting between crops.

Along the coast of Cape Breton the family is still central to the way of life. Unlike most large urban centres in Canada where separation of the family unit seems a prerequisite of adulthood, in Cheticamp, St. Joseph du Moine, Belle Cote and most of the communities along the Trail there are many homes where two, three and more generations have been raised under one roof. A son may often work alongside his father in the fields or on the boats and a newly married couple build their house on the land next to their parents. This tightly-knit way of life, the family pride and trust it engenders, becomes the basic strength of the island communities and the main reason for their survival over the years.

At Belle Cote where the Trail heads inland away from the sea, the traveller is taken into yet another physical environment. The softly rolling hills, and leisurely streams of the Margaree Valley could be an anti-climax after the rugged shoreline and pounding seas of the coast but instead, the traveller is charmed and soothed. The small farms and villages set in the quiet fields seem to welcome him back as he nears the end of his journey.

This valley is said to have been named by the French settlers after the wildflower called the Marguerite which is common to the area. Still preponderantly an Acadian culture, the region has never been prosperous and there are many derelict houses and broken-down barns. But if not rich in worldly goods, this part of Cape Breton is a fisherman's paradise and during the season the river and streams are busy with sportsmen trying to break the previous years' records. Such is the pride of the local people in their river harvest that an old school house has been converted into a salmon museum where even an unenthusiastic angler can enjoy learning the story of man's battle with the great fish.

When I first stopped at the little picnic site on the shores of the O'Law lakes, the mist was heavy on the crest of the hills and a light rain rustled the leaves of the overhanging trees. On the trunk of one of the trees were the initials of lovers enclosed in the traditional carved heart. Why, I wondered did I feel so at home here, so peaceful and refreshed? I knew I must return and later, on another trip, I did. In the light of dusk I walked along the shore, jumping from rock to rock and hanging onto the low boughs of the trees for balance. Eating a locally caught lobster at one of the picnic tables, I felt very much an islander and almost as if I had arrived two hundred years before, eager to explore and befriend the beautiful landscape.

'S e Ceap Breatainn tir mo ghraidh,
  Tir nan craobh, 's nam beanntan ard';
'S e Ceap Breatainn tir mo ghraidh,
  Tir is aillidh leinn air thalamh.

Cape Breton is the land of my love,
  The land of trees and high mountains.
Cape Breton is the land of my love;
  We deem it the most beautiful land on earth.

Dan Alex MacDonald
Framboise

Index

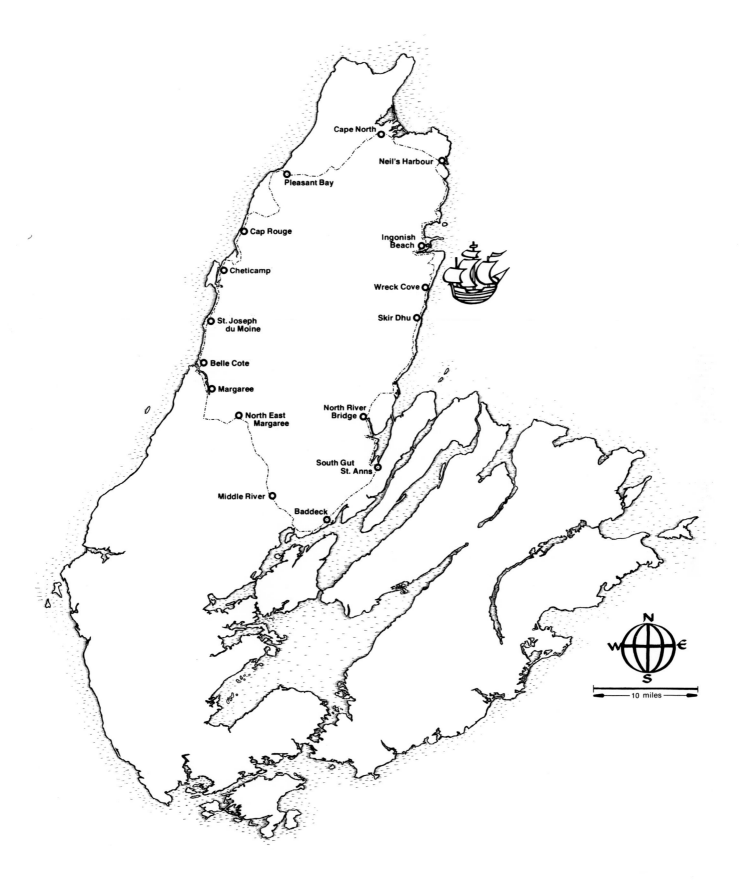

Cape North

Neil's Harbour

Pleasant Bay

Cap Rouge

Cheticamp

Ingonish
Beach

St. Joseph
du Moine

Wreck Cove

Skir Dhu

Belle Cote

Margaree

North East
Margaree

North River
Bridge

South Gut
St. Anns

Middle River

Baddeck

N
W E
S

10 miles